THE FIFTY BEST

HISTORIC AMERICAN HOUSES

COLONIAL AND FEDERAL

NOW FURNISHED AND OPEN TO THE PUBLIC

by

RALPH E. CARPENTER, JR.

WARNER HOUSE *Portsmouth, N. H.*

A MOWBRA HALL PRESS BOOK

E. P. DUTTON & COMPANY, INC.

NEW YORK · 1955

MONTMORENCI STAIRHALL *Winterthur Museum*

FOREWORD

Forty years ago, when I first bought woodwork from tumble-down old houses for my Southampton house, and a few years later, when I secured interiors from houses situated on some inlet of the Chesapeake Bay, or overlooking the Delaware River, or in some Virginia back-water village, or on the main street of a staid New England town, my first purpose was to save the paneling for posterity. Too often in our country the beauty and the historic significance of our early architecture have been overlooked until too late—the building gone, the paneling used for firewood. Through these forty years, my feeling has grown stronger and stronger that only through proper preservation could we keep a true picture of our colonial past—how our ancestors lived, what they built, what they had, and how they used what they had—and that only through keeping a true picture and understanding of it can we arrive today at the sense of values and the pride in fine workmanship and real worth that our forefathers had.

The preservation of the fifty houses shown in this book will enable one to visualize two hundred years of our growth and development, for in them we see another use of our old houses, in that they serve as a background for the objects which our ancestors had and used and enjoyed. Americans have for generations treasured family heirlooms, such as old portraits, furniture, and silver. Although these things are in themselves both beautiful and interesting, they seem to me to have a great deal more significance when seen as an integral part of the house. When we see them in their original settings, and against a background in which they were originally used, they mean more; there they seem to tell their whole story, not only of how they were used, but also of the kind of people who created and used them.

I have always been fascinated to visit old houses. Looking back on my own collecting days, I am happy to see that others were gaining knowledge and inspiration from our fine old houses, and collections were being preserved in various parts of the country. This book will serve a useful purpose in providing the visitor with advance information about each of the fifty old houses described in it, and as a source of knowledge for that group of people who, in ever-increasing numbers, are visiting old houses, for both education and enjoyment.

April 25, 1955   *Henry Francis du Pont*

CONTENTS

COLONIAL AMERICA TODAY

In this year of 1955 it is difficult for us to visualize the magnitude and appearance of Colonial America. Since 1765, our population has increased from 1,800,000 to 160,000,000. The city of Detroit, as of today, is large enough to have contained everyone who lived at that time in the thirteen colonies. As for cities in 1765, there were only five large enough to be classed as such, Philadelphia, New York, Boston, Charleston, S. C., and Newport, R. I., having populations of 30,000, 18,000, 15,500, 10,000, and 8,000 respectively. There were in New England some 500 towns with an average population of 1,000, practically all white. Almost two thirds of the white colonists and about 350,000 colored lived south of New York. Virginia was the most populous of all the colonies.

Families were large and several generations usually lived together. If we assume that each house sheltered on the average a family of ten, and records indicate this might be a pretty good guess, then we can assume that in 1765 approximately 140,000 houses were standing, some new and some already 100 years old. Since then many have burned, many have been allowed to decay; but most of those that are no longer with us have been demolished and replaced by newer structures, until today there are probably fewer than five out of every hundred still standing.

If nothing had happened during recent years to slow down this rate of destruction, our grandchildren would have regarded a Colonial dwelling in much the same way that we look upon a square-rigged ship, for all practical purposes an extinct species! Exaggeration? Consider New York City. How many Colonial structures remain intact today? The Jumel Mansion and the Dyckman House plus Fraunces Tavern and St. Paul's Church. Four out of maybe 1500 or 2000 standing on Manhattan Island in 1765! In other sections the rate has been slower but until recently headed toward the same result.

Fortunately, a movement which began about a hundred years ago, when the Mount Vernon Ladies Association of the Union raised $200,000 to save Mount Vernon, but which gained momentum at a snail's pace, has, during the past twenty-five years, picked up speed. From Maine to Virginia individuals and societies have been preserving the best of what was left. Fine houses have been restored and provided with appropriate furniture. Sometimes the house had to be moved to a new location as in the case of Wilton and Cedar Grove. Sometimes the house could not be moved, so one or more of the rooms were moved, and set up as in the Winterthur Museum and the American Wing of the Metropolitan.

During this period, many individuals have diligently sought out fine examples of Colonial furniture, silver, paintings and all the other collectables and have furnished the rooms or placed them in galleries and in museums, such as the Karolik Collection in the Boston Museum and the Garvan Collection at Yale. Finally, whole areas containing numbers of buildings have been restored as in the case of Williamsburg and Deerfield.

Altogether much more than $100,000,000 has been devoted to this program. The amount of study and research necessary to do it authentically and in good taste has been fantastic. Much is still going on and will continue to go on, adding each year more houses, more collections and more restorations.

In the meantime the traveler who finds relaxation, enjoyment, and education by visiting such places, needs assistance. Briefly, where are the best examples? How do I get there? When are they open? What will I see when I get there? What does it cost? The purpose of this publication is to answer these questions.

A selection of fifty houses now furnished and open to the public has been made on the basis of a combined "score" of historical association, architectural interest, and the furnishing of the interior. In a brief commentary on each category, the reader may discover the relative importance of each for any given house.

Because those who are interested in historical houses usually have collateral interests in furniture, silver, tools, glass and other classifications, a list of institutions offering exhibitions in these fields has been added.

The author is not unmindful that in listing these houses and institutions, some that should have been included may have been either overlooked or misjudged. Such errors of omission will receive utmost consideration in subsequent printings and suggestions will gratefully be received and assiduously evaluated. _R. E. C., Jr._

NATHAN HALE HOMESTEAD—1776
South Coventry, Connecticut

OPEN   May 15 to November 1—Daily except Monday
10:00 A.M. to 5:00 P.M.

ADMISSION   Adults   .50

MAIL ADDRESS   Connecticut Antiquarian and Landmark Society
c/o Mrs. Lillian Cogan
Farmington, Connecticut

DIRECTIONS   Approximately 15 miles due east of Hartford.
Take Alternate Route 44 to Coventry, then
right on Route 31 to South Coventry.

HISTORICAL COMMENT

The house in which Nathan Hale was born on June 6, 1755 stood on property not far from the present building and is marked by a tablet inscribed with his immortal words, "I only regret that I have but one life to lose for my country". The building that stands today was built in 1776 by Nathan's father and in it his brother taught school. The blackboard still remains on the wall of one of the rooms. After attending Yale, Nathan entered the Army and was captured by the English while attempting to obtain information in New York City and executed as a spy in 1776, the same year his father built this house. The Hale family lived in the homestead until 1832.

ARCHITECTURAL FEATURES

The house is typical of the houses of the period in rural New England. The parlor has paneling which has a degree of sophistication appropriate to the house. The house typifies what a successful farmer wanted as a comfortable home.

FURNISHINGS

The house is furnished throughout with furniture and fabrics which would have been used in a house in this locality. Not all of the houses in Colonial America were mansions and it is here that one can see how the great "middle class" of the northern colonies lived. In fact, while not a mansion compared to those houses of the wealthy merchants along the coast or the planters of Virginia, it was for a time designated as such by the people of the neighborhood whose pursuit of agriculture produced only a meager living. The house, as would have been the case in the eighteenth century, has a number of beds, each being in a different style, each authentic.

BUTTOLPH-WILLIAMS HOUSE—1692
Broad Street, Wethersfield, Connecticut

OPEN   From May 15th to October 15th
Every day (except Monday) from 12:30 to 4:30 P.M.

ADMISSION   Adults   .50   Children with an adult   .25
Special rates to organizations and schools

MAIL ADDRESS   Antiquarian and Landmark Society of Conn-
necticut, Inc.
Box 208, Hartford, Connecticut

DIRECTIONS   Follow Main Street and turn at Marsh Street to
Broad Street

HISTORICAL COMMENT

Joseph Webb built the house in 1752 when he was 25 and lived there with his wife Mehitabel Nott for 9 years. After his death his widow married Silas Deane, who preceded Franklin in Paris as a representative of the Continental Congress. Deane built the house next door and Joseph Webb, Jr., and his wife moved into the Webb House. The house's most historic role was played in May of 1781 when Washington and Gen. Knox, who later became our first Secretary of War, met the Count de Rochambeau and his aide the Marquis de Chastellux here. Washington came from New Windsor on the Hudson and de Rochambeau from Newport, R. I. The purpose of the meeting was to plan the campaign which terminated with success at Yorktown.

ARCHITECTURAL FEATURES

It may be that the ell of the house was built in 1678. The house, a fine example of the period, is now painted white but when Washington visited it, it was red. The front porch is a later addition. An interesting construction feature concerns the summer beams (the term comes from the French and denotes that which carries the load). In the north parlor the beam runs from the fireplace wall to the outside wall, as is usual. In the south parlor, it is parallel to the chimney wall. The house contains much fine paneling.

FURNISHINGS

It is well furnished with eighteenth-century furniture, china, and glass. Some of the Webb family items are included. The collection of textiles, both early and late, is outstanding and of great interest, as is also the gentleman's library on the first floor.

DUMBARTON HOUSE—1805
2715 Q Street, N.W., Washington, D. C.

OPEN   Every day except Sundays and holidays
From 10:00 A.M. to 5:00 P.M.

ADMISSION   Free

MAIL ADDRESS   2715 Q Street N. W.
Washington, D. C.
Phone De. 2–0028

DIRECTIONS   Take bus marked either Glover Park or MacArthur Boulevard. Buses may be boarded at Woodward and Lathrop or at the Statler Hotel.

HISTORICAL COMMENT

The property on which Dumbarton House stands is part of what was originally a large grant of land which also included the site of Dumbarton Oaks, scene of the 1944 political conference which preceded the founding of the United Nations in San Francisco in 1946.

The construction of the house was begun by George Beall shortly after the middle of the eighteenth century but the house, as it stands today, was not completed until 1805. It was lived in during its early years by Ninian Beall and served as a residence without interruption, until acquired by the National Society of Colonial Dames in the 1930's.

ARCHITECTURAL FEATURES

The house is an outstanding example of the Federal style in the Middle States. The frieze of the downstairs rooms is notable. In 1917 it became necessary to remove the house to make room for Q Street and at that time, the center section was moved intact, the wings were reassembled.

FURNISHINGS

The furnishings, provided largely by gift, make this one of the best examples of a Federal interior. One of the recent acquisitions is the Peale protrait of the Stoddert children. Stoddert was one of the founders of Georgetown. On the upper floor is a museum room containing glass, silver, and china.

LADY PEPPERRELL HOUSE—1760
Kittery Point, Maine

OPEN   From June 15th to September 15th
Monday through Friday   10:00 A.M. to 12:00 Noon
2:00 P.M. to 4:00 P.M.

ADMISSION   Adults   .50

MAIL ADDRESS   Society for the Preservation of New England
Antiquities
141 Cambridge Street, Boston 14, Mass.

DIRECTIONS   On Route 103, 4 miles from Portsmouth, N. H.

HISTORICAL COMMENT

This house was built in 1760 by the widow of Sir William Pepperrell. He led a victorious expedition to Louisburg during the French and Indian War (1745) and became the first American to be knighted by the Crown. Sir William was called "the Piscataway trader". His wealth, estimated at 250,000 pounds sterling, would make him the richest man in the Colonies. He raised and financed a whole regiment at the time of the Louisburg Expedition.

ARCHITECTURAL FEATURES

Originally the house did not have the side piazzas although some early houses did, Copley's house in Boston for one. In order to have room for inside shutters, the window trim, caps and sills project outside of the clapboards. The beach stone walk leading to the entrance was found under heavy turf.

FURNISHINGS

Appropriate furnishings are being assembled with a view to restoring the interior to an appearance similar to that of the eighteenth century.

HAMMOND-HARWOOD HOUSE—1774
19 Maryland Avenue, Annapolis, Maryland

OPEN   Summer: Monday through Saturday 10 A.M. to 5 P.M.
Sunday 2 to 5 P.M.
Winter: Monday through Saturday 10 A.M. to 4 P.M.
Sunday 1 to 4 P.M.

ADMISSION   Adults .50   Children .25
School groups .20   Groups over 25 .35

MAIL ADDRESS   Hammond-Harwood House Association, Inc.
19 Maryland Ave., Annapolis, Maryland

DIRECTIONS   On Maryland Avenue one block from the Naval
Academy

HISTORICAL COMMENT

John Hammond, 1643–1707, was appointed a Commissioner to lay out the town of Annapolis. John's great grandson, Matthias Hammond, who built this house in 1774, studied law and in 1773 at the age of 25 was elected to the Provincial Assembly. In June of 1774 he was on the Committee of Correspondence, and in 1775 signed the Proclamation of the Freeman of Maryland. In 1776, still active in patriotic affairs and completing his town house, his name suddenly disappeared from any records until his death November 16, 1786. However, he never married and it appears that his fiancée eloped with another man just before they were to wed and occupy the house, and his bitterness prevented him from ever living there.

ARCHITECTURAL FEATURES

William Buckland, who had come over from London earlier to design Gunston Hall for George Mason, to whom he was indentured for four years to pay off his passage, drew the plans. Meat, drink, washing, lodging, and 20 pounds per year were paid for his service. When he finished, he was still only 25 and spent the next 12 years practicing his profession in Virginia before going to Annapolis. He and Matthias Hammond worked out the plans of the Hammond-Harwood house, and his portrait, at the Yale Art Gallery by C. W. Peale, shows the floor plan and front elevation of the Hammond House.

It is presumed that the plans were completed prior to Buckland's death in November 1774. The house had been started in March of the same year. At least we know that the finished house as it stands today is evidence of a superlative accomplishment.

FURNISHINGS

The furnishings of the house today are as carefully and as expertly done as the house itself. There is little else one can add.

CHASE–LLOYD HOUSE—1769
Maryland Avenue and King George Street
Annapolis, Maryland

OPEN   Every day 10:00 A.M. to 12:00 noon; 2:00 to 5:00 P.M.

ADMISSION   .25 per person

MAIL ADDRESS   The Chase House
22 Maryland Avenue, Annapolis, Maryland

DIRECTIONS   It is located within one block of the entrance to
the Naval Academy.

HISTORICAL COMMENT

This house was begun in 1769 by Samuel Chase, one of the Maryland signers of the Declaration of Independence, and completed by Governor Edward Lloyd. In 1802 it was the scene of the marriage between Mary Tayloe Lloyd and Francis Scott Key, author of the Star Spangled Banner. In the year 1886 Mrs. Hester Ann Chase Ridout (a descendant of Samuel Chase), who lived here, devised it in perpetuity as a Home for Aged and Infirm Women.

ARCHITECTURAL FEATURES

An imposing three-story brick mansion, it has all of the attributes of good colonial architecture of the period in Maryland. The interior is of the highest quality of workmanship and decoration. The hardware is superb.

FURNISHINGS

The furnishings have been suited to the use to which the house has been put.

HARRISON GRAY OTIS HOUSE—1795
141 Cambridge Street, Boston, Massachusetts

OPEN   Monday through Friday 9:00 A.M. to 4:45 P.M.
Closed Saturday, Sunday and holidays

ADMISSION   .25

MAIL ADDRESS   Society for the Preservation of New England
Antiquities
141 Cambridge Street, Boston, Mass.

DIRECTIONS   Enter from Lynde Street.

HISTORICAL COMMENT

Harrison Gray Otis built this house in 1795. He was a lawyer, statesman, member of the U. S. House of Representatives and the Senate.

ARCHITECTURAL FEATURES

This fine house has often been attributed to Bulfinch, who designed the State House on Beacon Hill. The rooms contain outstanding examples of the interior architecture of the period, especially the mantlepieces and wood trim. The Society's Museum is in the rear and contains many architectural relics of Colonial New England.

FURNISHINGS

Three sets of historic French wallpaper have been hung on the walls of two rooms of the second floor. The collection of furniture of the eighteenth century is being added to each year and at present includes many fine pieces.

JOHN WHIPPLE HOUSE—1640
Ipswich, Massachusetts

OPEN   Tuesday through Saturday 10 A.M. to 5 P.M.
Sundays 1 to 5 P.M.   Closed Mondays
Closed every day November 1 to April 1

ADMISSION .50   Children under 12, free

MAIL ADDRESS   Ipswich Historical Society
Ipswich, Massachusetts

DIRECTIONS   Approximately 30 miles north of Boston turn
right off Route 133 and go east 5 miles.

HISTORICAL COMMENT

John Fawn built in 1640 a two-story, two-room house with a steep-pitched thatched roof and casement windows. Two years later, Elder John Whipple was living there and it was owned and occupied by successive generations for two hundred years. In 1898 the Ipswich Historical Society bought and restored the house.

ARCHITECTURAL FEATURES

In 1670 the east half was added to the original structure and a further addition was made sometime after 1700 when the lean-to was constructed; the interior has all the attributes of a fine seventeenth-century house: heavy chamfered oak and tamarack beams, gunstock posts, vertical wall boarding with "shadow moulding", clay and brick filled walls, and enormous fireplaces. Houses of such an early date have become extremely rare.

FURNISHINGS

Over the years many old Ipswich families have contributed to the furnishings which are of both the seventeenth and eighteenth centuries.

JEREMIAH LEE MANSION—1768
Washington Street, Marblehead, Massachusetts

OPEN   From May 15th through October 15th   9:00 A.M. to
5:00 P.M.
Closed Sundays

ADMISSION   Adults .50   Children   .30

MAIL ADDRESS   Mrs. Elbridge Girdler, Curator
13 Darling Street, Marblehead, Mass.

DIRECTIONS   Follow Washington Street until it intersects with
Hooper Street.

HISTORICAL COMMENT

This house was built in 1768 by Col. Jeremiah Lee, a prosperous merchant prince, whose ships sailed the seven seas. Always active in civic affairs, he attended an important meeting in Lexington on the eve of the Revolution and catching "lung fever" he met an early death. In 1792 his widow sold the house to Chief Justice Sewall who sold it in 1804 to the newly organized bank. For 105 years it was used as a bank building and a residence for the banker. In 1824 the Marquis de Lafayette was entertained by the people of the town at a dinner given in the rooms over the bank. In 1909 the Marblehead Historical Society bought the mansion.

ARCHITECTURAL FEATURES

Without doubt the Jeremiah Lee house is one of the finest examples of New England Colonial architecture which was largely inspired by the English Georgian. Built in 1768 at a reputed cost of 50,000 pounds, Lee's own ships brought mahogany for the grand staircase from San Domingo, materials for construction and decoration and wallpaper from England. The room to the left of the entrance is perhaps the finest paneled room in New England. Swan's *British Architect*, Plate 51, furnished the design for the over mantel.

FURNISHINGS

The furnishing has been meticulously attended to and includes furniture of superb quality. The marble-top tables, window hangings and beds are outstanding.

KING HOOPER MANSION—1728
8 Hooper Street, Marblehead, Massachusetts

OPEN   Daily except Monday 2:00 to 5:00 P.M.

ADMISSION   Adults   .30

MAIL ADDRESS   8 Hooper Street, Marblehead, Massachusetts
(Marblehead Arts Association)

DIRECTIONS   Follow Washington Street to its intersection with
Hooper Street.

HISTORICAL COMMENT

Greenfield Hooper, a tallow chandler, bought in 1727 the land on which the mansion stands and built the five story building facing the garden. Robert (King) Hooper, the son, married four times, had eleven children, and became the wealthiest merchant in Marblehead. He added in 1745 the three story building in the front of the property. Civic-minded, he gave the town a fire engine in 1751, and helped establish the first academy. Robert, Jr., married the daughter of General Glover. Lafayette, an old comrade in arms of Glover, visited her in 1824.

ARCHITECTURAL FEATURES

Built within a few years of the Royal House, the Hooper House has much the same style. The three storied facade and doorway of each have much in common. Inside there is a large ballroom on the third floor.

FURNISHINGS

The furnishings have been gathered with a view to eventually furnishing it completely in the style that it was originally.

ISAAC ROYALL HOUSE—1732
Medford, Massachusetts

OPEN   Open daily except Monday and Friday from May 1st
to October 1st   2:00 to 5:00 P.M.

ADMISSION   Adults .50   Groups of 20 or more .35 each
Children .25   Groups of 20 or more .15 each

MAIL ADDRESS   Mr. Arthur L. Finney
15 George Street, Medford, Massachusetts

DIRECTIONS   Medford is about 5 miles from downtown Boston
on Route 38.

HISTORICAL COMMENT

The property on which the Royall house stands was originally granted in 1631 to Gov. John Winthrop. In 1732 Col. Isaac Royall, a wealthy merchant from Antigua purchased and rebuilt the house as it now stands, together with quarters for his 27 slaves. From the time of his father's death in 1739 Isaac Royall, Jr., lived in the house, until he departed for Halifax with other Loyalists. In 1775 the estate was confiscated and General Stark made it his headquarters. Generals Washington, Lee and Sullivan met here often. Col. Cary, Washington's aide, leased the house from 1782–84. In 1806 the Government returned the estate to the Royall heirs and money from the sale of part of the land helped found Harvard Law School. It was purchased and restored in 1908 by the Royall House Association.

ARCHITECTURAL FEATURES

The exterior is one of the most interesting of all the three story New England house. The most striking feature of the facade are the windows which, together with the entablatures above the head and bibs below the sills, give emphasis to the vertical lines of the house. The design is similar to that used in some of the English houses made of stone, such as Stoneleigh Priory in Warwickshire. Inside, the house incorporates portions of an earlier house built by Gov. John Winthrop prior to 1649. Because of the low ceilings of the earlier house, the present one has an informal atmosphere in spite of its fine paneling and elaborate staircase.

FURNISHINGS

The house is completely furnished with a mixture of American and English furniture of the eighteenth century.

THE ASHLEY HOUSE—c. 1733
Old Deerfield, Massachusetts

OPEN   Weekdays 9:30 A.M. to 12:00 Noon   1:30 to 4:30 P.M.
Sunday 1:30 to 4:30 P.M.

ADMISSION   Individual tickets   .50
A ticket for this house and 4 others $1.50

MAIL ADDRESS   Information Center
Hall Tavern, Deerfield, Mass.

DIRECTIONS   Deerfield is 15 miles north of Northampton,
Mass. on Route 5.

HISTORICAL COMMENT

The village parson, Jonathan Ashley, bought this house in 1733 for 35 pounds. It had been built by John Wells. Ashley, a member of a wealthy Westfield family, came to the pastorate shortly after his graduation from Yale. He married Dorothy Williams and together they raised a family of nine children. The parson, an outspoken Tory, remained in Deerfield during the Revolution, dying there in 1780.

ARCHITECTURAL FEATURES

The Ashley house remained the family homestead until 1859 when it was moved to the rear of the property and converted to a tobacco barn. Now restored and returned to its original location, it "embodies the salient points of good Deerfield houses, unpainted clapboards, narrow, unshuttered windows, and a rich Connecticut Valley Doorway" which, while not original, represents a type distinctive of the region.

FURNISHINGS

The furnishings have been selected so as to be consistent with Parson Ashley's taste and position. An original Ashley piece, a dressing table in the north chamber, has "set a standard for the other furniture in the house". Many fine Connecticut Valley pieces are included.

ASA STEBBENS HOUSE—1799
Old Deerfield Village, Massachusetts

OPEN   Daily 9:30 A.M. to 12 Noon   1:30 to 4:30 P.M.

ADMISSION   Individual tickets   .50
                       A ticket for this house and 4 others $1.50

MAIL ADDRESS   Information Center, Hall Tavern
                        Deerfield, Massachusetts

DIRECTIONS   Deerfield is 15 miles north of Northampton Mass.
                    on Route 5.

HISTORICAL COMMENT

Around 1750 Joseph Stebbens, Sr., was probably living in what is now the ell in the rear. During the Revolution, Deerfield became a center for beef cattle and Stebbens made the most of an opportunity to furnish the troops with shoulder straps. Asa apparently inherited his father's savings and then went into partnership with his brother, Joseph, Jr., who had so distinguished himself at Bunker Hill and Saratoga, that Deerfield Village granted him tax exemption on his grist mill. Success made it possible for Asa to erect in 1799 the house which now stands, with bricks that were made on the property.

ARCHITECTURAL FEATURES

The restrained severity of the exterior, typical of the Connecticut Valley, relies almost entirely on a belt course at the second floor level and a rustication of the doorway for its decorative detail. In the front hall the handsome paneling and fanlight of the front door, together with the trim of the inside doors and cornice, furnish a fine example of rural Federal interior architecture.

FURNISHINGS

While the furnishings are predominantly late eighteenth century, they do include earlier examples which could have belonged to earlier generations in the Stebbens family. The furnishing of the house is complete and on a very high quality level. For example, in the south parlor an Aubusson rug blends with the pink walls. In the center of the room a drop leaf table is set with china. Over the sofa hangs a portrait painted by Gilbert Stuart in 1775. A crystal chandelier hangs from the ceiling. A magnificent mirror hangs between windows hung with India mull curtains. A secretary-bookcase displays fine china. Once considered the showplace of the village, the Stebbens House is again in full bloom.

ADAMS "OLD HOUSE"—1731
Adams Street, Quincy, Massachusetts

OPEN   Every day from May 10 to November 10
9:00 A.M. to 5:15 P.M.

ADMISSION   Adults   .25
Children under 12 free when accompanied by responsible adults

MAIL ADDRESS   Adams National Historic Site
Adams Street, Quincy, Massachusetts

DIRECTIONS   Approximately 8 miles from Boston, the house is on State Route 135 and adjacent to State Route 3. There is frequent train and bus service from Boston.

John Adams, while Minister to Great Britain in 1787, bought the house and moved in the next year. During his Presidency he built the ell. An active patriot, he was largely responsible for the selection of Washington as Commander-in-chief; was one of the Committee of Five that drafted the Declaration of Independence; a Commissioner to France in 1778; Minister to Holland in 1783; negotiated, with Franklin and Jay, the Treaty of Peace ending the American Revolution; in 1785 he was Minister to Great Britain; with Franklin and Jefferson he selected E Pluribus Unum (one out of many) for our National Motto; Vice President during Washington's two terms; elected President in 1796, retired in 1801, and died July 4, 1826.

He had lived to see his son, John Quincy Adams, elected President in 1825. The son who had been graduated from Harvard in 1787, was Minister to Holland in 1794; Minister to Prussia in 1796; U. S. Senator in 1803; Minister to Russia in 1809, and signed the Treaty of Ghent in 1814 ending the War of 1812. He was Minister to Great Britain before becoming Secretary of State in 1817 and had taken an active part in establishing the Monroe Doctrine. After his term as President, he served 17 years in Congress, dying on the floor of the House in 1848 at the age of 81. Other generations of the Adams family lived on in the "Old House" until in 1927 the Adams Memorial Society was formed to preserve it, and in 1946 transferred title to the United States.

ARCHITECTURAL FEATURES

The history of its occupants overshadows the architectural importance. It does, however, show how early houses grew to accommodate its owners' needs. The oldest part was built in 1731 by Major Leonard Vassall. John Adams during his Presidency (1796–1800) built the large gabled ell. In 1836 John Q. added the passage along the north side. In 1869 Charles Francis Adams added 30 feet to the kitchen ell and the stone library.

FURNISHINGS

The furnishings all represent the contributions of successive generations who lived there.

HOUSE OF SEVEN GABLES—1668
54 Turner Street, Salem, Massachusetts

OPEN   Every day in the year (except Thanksgiving and Christmas) from 10:00 A.M. to 5:00 P.M.

ADMISSION   Adults .75   Students .50
Children 8 to 12   .30

MAILING ADDRESS   House of Seven Gables
54 Turner Street, Salem, Massachusetts
Telephone Salem 0991

DIRECTIONS   Turn off Route 1A at Derby Street and go east to Turner Street, and turn right one block.

HISTORICAL COMMENT

The house was built in 1668 by John Turner and was owned by the Turner family for more than a century. Then for another hundred years it was owned by the Ingersoll family and during that period it was frequented by a kinsman, Nathaniel Hawthorne, who found it an inspiration for his novel. Since 1910 the house has been owned by the House of Seven Gables Settlement Association and all profits are used for social welfare work.

ARCHITECTURAL FEATURES

The style of the house is typical of the seventeenth century in New England with the characteristic steep roof, second floor overhang and weathered clapboards. The interior contains in some rooms fine paneling added during the eighteenth century and a secret staircase. The parlor cupboard with its arched and paneled door, scalloped shelves and shell-carved dome forms a part of a most satisfying paneled wall. The generous use of bolection molding firmly establishes its fine design.

FURNISHINGS

The house contains many of the original pieces of furniture, accumulated by the owners over the many years of successive occupancy. Because of Nathaniel Hawthorne's association with the house, many items related to him are to be seen. In going through the house do not be diverted from the early paintings and furniture by the later acquisitions.

PINGREE HOUSE—1804
128 Essex Street, Salem, Massachusetts

OPEN   Daily except Sundays and holidays
9 to 11:15 A.M. and 2 to 4:00 P.M.

ADMISSION   Adults .50   Children free when with an adult

MAIL ADDRESS   Essex Institute
Salem, Massachusetts

DIRECTIONS   128 Essex Street, next door to Essex Institute

HISTORICAL COMMENT

This house was designed and built by Samuel McIntire in 1804 for Capt. John Gardner, a prosperous sea captain. Thirty years later it was sold to David Pingree, whose son, David, Jr., was born and died in the house. Ownership remained in the Pingree family for almost a century before it was conveyed to the Essex Institute. David, Jr., had been Senior Vice President of the Institute.

ARCHITECTURAL FEATURES

The house is a three story brick mansion with an "L" in the rear. A broad band of white marble marks each floor on the outside walls, and a balustrade runs around the roof at the eaves. Inside the spacious hall has a fine stairway, with white pine balusters of Chippendale style. The fireplace mantels and wood trim of the doors and windows represent McIntire at his best. Many of the mantels and the balusters of the stairs were replaced during the middle of the nineteenth century with designs then in vogue. Fortunately they were preserved and are now returned to their original positions in the house. The wood carving of the mantels is exquisite and these alone would make a visit to the house well worthwhile.

FURNISHINGS

The house is furnished throughout as though it had been lived in by successive generations. Much of the furniture is of Salem origin and is in the Sheraton and Hepplewhite style. The hangings on the windows and beds are exceptional.

THE DERBY HOUSE—1761–62
Derby Street (opp. Derby Wharf), Salem, Massachusetts

OPEN Every day 10 A.M. to 5 P.M.
   Closed on holidays falling between Nov. 11 and Feb. 22

ADMISSION .25 Children under 12 admitted free when
   accompanied by adults
   Servicemen in uniform admitted free

MAIL ADDRESS Salem Maritime National Historic Site
   Custom House, Derby Street
   Salem, Massachusetts

DIRECTIONS Turn off Route 1A and go two blocks on
   Derby Street.

HISTORICAL COMMENT

The Derby House was erected in 1761–62 by Capt. Richard Derby for his son Elias Hasket Derby who married in 1761 Elizabeth Crowninshield and lived with her in the house until 1777 or 1778, during which time seven children were born. Earlier, in 1757, Elizabeth's brother George had married Mary Derby, oldest daughter of Capt. Richard. The Derby house later became the home of the Nichols family, and George Nichols, who later occupied the McIntire Peirce-Nichols house, was born in the Derby house. Later, Capt. Henry Prince, a Master in the Derby Fleet, sailed the first American vessel, the *Astrea* II, to the Philippines in 1796. Prince's daughter married Henry Ropes. Members of the Ropes family lived here until 1873 when it fell on evil days until rescued by the Society for the Preservation of New England Antiquities.

ARCHITECTURAL FEATURES

The design of the house is a good example of the later use of the gambrel-roof, not as large, it is 43 feet wide and 27 feet deep, nor as lavish as its predecessors of this type, such as the Warner, Webb, or Nichols-Wanton-Hunter house, but very satisfying in proportion and appearance. In 1928 the Society for the Preservation of New England Antiquities performed under the direction of George Francis Dow essential restoration work, removing later mantel pieces, returning doorways to their proper size, patching up stove-pipe holes in the paneling, etc. After 1938 the National Park Service restored the original colors and performed other needed restoration.

FURNISHINGS

The furnishing of the house with pieces dating 1750–1775 or earlier has been done with excellent taste. The pastel portraits by Benjamin Blyth done while the Derby family was still there in 1776 are worthy of note.

THE PEIRCE-NICHOLS HOUSE—1782
80 Federal Street, Salem, Massachusetts

OPEN   Tuesdays through Saturdays 2 to 5 P.M.
Also open by appointment
Closed Sundays, Mondays and holidays

ADMISSION   Adults .50
Children free when accompanied by adult

MAIL ADDRESS   Director, Essex Institute, Salem, Massachusetts

DIRECTIONS   From Salem Common take Essex Street to North
Street, turn right on North one block to Federal
Street, turn left on Federal

HISTORICAL COMMENT

Jerathmeel Peirce bought the land March 6, 1779, and built the house sometime between this date and 1782. On November 22, 1801, George Nichols, who was born in the Derby House, married Sally Peirce in the "great eastern room" and they subsequently lived in the house.

ARCHITECTURAL FEATURES

This house is probably the best known of all the surviving houses attributed to Samuel McIntire. Subsequent to 1782 changes were made in the interior. Just prior to the marriage of his daughter, Jerathmeel Peirce changed the interior woodwork and the furnishings of the east parlor. At the same time the hall and the bedroom above the east parlor were changed to the style then in vogue. The porches and the woodwork of the west parlor and chamber and backstairs belong to the original house.

FURNISHINGS

The furnishing has been superbly done and contains some of the pieces original to the house.

OLD IRON MASTER'S HOUSE—c. 1640
235 Central Street, Saugus, Massachusetts

OPEN April 19th to December 1st Every day except Monday
9:00 A.M. to 4:00 P.M.

ADMISSION Adults .50 Children .25

MAIL ADDRESS Saugus Ironworks Restoration
235 Central Street, Saugus, Massachusetts.

DIRECTIONS Driving north on U. S. Route 1 turn right on
Main Street of Saugus and follow signs. Driving south on U. S. 1, turn left on Route 129, and
follow signs. Saugus is 10 miles north of Boston.

HISTORICAL COMMENT

The house is believed to have been built between 1636 and 1642. Originally owned by Thomas Dexter, it was acquired by the Company of Undertakers for the Iron Works as a residence for the iron master. After the Iron Works were abandoned Samuel Appleton foreclosed the mortgage on the Iron Works in 1688 and sold it to William Taylor. In 1712 it was sold to Daniel Mansfield, and remained in that family until 1840. During the Revolution it was owned by Thomas Mansfield and became the center of town life and political activity. After passing through numerous hands, it was bought by Wallace Nutting, and restored.

ARCHITECTURAL FEATURES

The Old Iron Master's House is typical of the houses built during the seventeenth century: a steep roof with numerous gables; second floor overhang; leaded casement windows and pilastered chimney. Adjoining the house is the restored iron works, the first successful iron works in America, which operated from 1643 to 1675. There is also a museum containing many relics which were excavated during the restoration.

FURNISHINGS

The house contains many seventeenth century pieces; a court cupboard, a wainsot chair dated 1660, a 1655 fireback from Kittery, Maine. By careful planning the spirit of early Colonial times has been caught to a remarkable degree.

GORE PLACE—1804
Main Street, Waltham, Massachusetts

OPEN   Tuesday through Saturday 10 A.M. to 5 P.M.
Winter 10 A.M. to 4 P.M.
Sunday 2 to 5 P.M.   Closed on Monday

ADMISSION   .50

MAIL ADDRESS   Director, Gore Place Society
Waltham 54, Massachusetts

DIRECTIONS   On Route 20, halfway between Watertown and
Waltham

Christopher Gore, builder and owner of Gore Place, was born in Boston, September 28, 1758. He entered Harvard at the age of 13, graduating in 1776. His father, a Tory, went to Halifax but the son served in the American Army. A lawyer, he became after the war the first U. S. Attorney in Massachusetts and also served as a Commissioner to England under the Jay Treaty, settling the claims of American citizens for spoliation.

After his return from England in 1804, he served as State Senator, State Representative, Governor of Massachusetts, President of the Massachusetts Historical Society, and Fellow and Overseer of Harvard College—to which he bequeathed $100,000, the largest bequest received by Harvard up to the time of his death, March 1, 1829.

ARCHITECTURAL FEATURES

A previous wooden house, which stood on the site of Gore Place, burned while its owner was in England, so when Christopher Gore returned from England in 1804, he brought with him plans attributed to the English architect, Sir John Soane (1753–1837). The house has 22 rooms and cost $23,000. Built of small pinkish brick, its style and appearance is closely related to that of the English country houses which were seldom copied in New England, being a type you would expect to find in Virginia. The eighteenth-century stables antedate the house. Seventy-six acres still remain of the original holdings.

FURNISHINGS

The house has been furnished through the efforts of the Gore Place Society.

GOVERNOR JOHN LANGDON MANSION—1784
143 Pleasant Street, Portsmouth, New Hampshire

OPEN   Monday through Saturday, 1 to 5 P.M.
Closed from middle of September to June 1st.

ADMISSION   Adults .50

MAIL ADDRESS   Society for the Preservation of New England
Antiquities
141 Cambridge Street
Boston, Massachusetts

DIRECTIONS   Turn off U. S. Route 1 at Pleasant Street and go
south to 143 Pleasant Street

HISTORICAL COMMENT

This splendid mansion was built in 1784 by John Langdon, one of the great leaders in the Revolution. He was five times Governor of New Hampshire and was the first President of the U. S. Senate. Acting President of the United States prior to the election of George Washington, he was the first to notify him of his election. During the war, John Langdon had pledged his entire fortune to the cause. Many were the visitors to his house, among them the Marquis de Chastellux in 1782, prior to the embarkation of his regiment for France from Portsmouth (they had marched from Williamsburg after Yorktown to New York, and then to Portsmouth), and in 1789 George Washington stayed here. Later, the exiled Louis Philippe of France and his brothers were guests.

ARCHITECTURAL FEATURES

Though its design is similar to other houses of the period in scale and magnificence, it is one of the best of its type. John Mead Howells properly described the house as a "magnificent example of the fully developed early American architecture. Such a house is popularly called a Colonial Mansion and as such, is dear to the hearts of Americans."

FURNISHINGS

The furnishings give the house a "lived in" look and are a mixture of American and English.

THE MOFFATT-LADD HOUSE—1763
Market Street, Portsmouth, New Hampshire

OPEN   Monday through Saturday 10 A.M. to 5 P.M.

ADMISSION   Adults .50

MAIL ADDRESS   Moffatt-Ladd House
Market Street, Portsmouth, New Hampshire

DIRECTIONS   Turn off U. S. 1 at Market Square and go north
on Market Street.

Capt. John Moffatt, aged 71, built this house for his only son, Samuel, at the time he married Sarah Catherine Mason, descendant of John Mason, friend of Myles Standish. Capt. John came on one of the King's Mast ships, stayed to make money as a merchant. Samuel failed in business in 1768 and fled to the West Indies. Stringent property laws (a stockbroker who "borrowed" money from a client without permission was *executed* in 1763) were in effect. Samuel's wife remained with the Captain until the third child was born.

Capt. Moffat bought the house at a creditors' auction and lived there until 1786, aged 94. Paul Revere brought a message from Boston on December 16, 1774, to Samuel Cutts, Moffat's brother-in-law, who lived next door. It precipitated the attack on Fort William & Mary, the first armed attack on Great Britain by the Colonists. Captain Moffat's son-in-law, General William Whipple, who signed the Declaration of Independence, lived in the house with him.

ARCHITECTURAL FEATURES

This house was the first of the three-story hip-roof type in Portsmouth. The segmental pediments of the ground floor windows and the swan-necked pediments on the second floor are a fine feature. The side windows have no pediments. The body of the house was originally pink putty and the quoins and balustrades were gray granite. The feature of the interior is the very large hall which is unique in New England houses. The Dufours wallpaper with its *vues d'Italie* is important.

FURNISHINGS

The furnishings have been assembled by the Colonial Dames of New Hampshire with a view to restoring its appearance to what it was at the time it was lived in in the eighteenth century.

WARNER HOUSE—c. 1716
Portsmouth, New Hampshire

OPEN   Monday through Saturday   10:00 A.M. to 5:00 P.M.
from June 10 to September 20.
Closed Sunday and holidays.

ADMISSION   Adults   .50   Children under 12 free
Special rate of .25 for parties of 15 or more.

MAIL ADDRESS   Mrs. E. T. Wendell
347 Thaxter Road, Portsmouth, N. H.

DIRECTIONS   From Market Square go toward the Memorial
Bridge via Daniels Street, two blocks to corner
of Chapel Street.

HISTORICAL COMMENT

Capt. Archbold MacPheadris came from Scotland and built the house between 1712 and 1723 at a cost of 6000 pounds, the equivalent today of something well over $200,000. He married Lt. Governor Wentworth's daughter, Sarah, and their daughter married the Hon. Jonathan Warner, a member of the King's Council. A lightning rod put up in 1762 under Dr. Benjamin Franklin's supervision still provides protection to the house. The house was occupied by collateral descendents of its past owner until 1931, when it was purchased by the Warner House Association.

ARCHITECTURAL FEATURES

This is the oldest brick house in Portsmouth and while claim is made that the brick came from Holland, it is more likely that the brick was of the type known as "Holland Brick" from its shape and size. Originally the roof was of a double peaked type with a deep valley between. Probably the snow and ice of Portsmouth accounted for the conversion to a gambrel roof. Underneath the old shingles can still be seen in place, one of the very few portions of Colonial shingled roofs extant. A section of the wall in the dining room retains the original marbleized paint and the rest of the room has been copied.

FURNISHINGS

Among the furnishings there are five portraits of the Warner family painted by Blackburn in 1761, some of which still hang in the rooms in which they were originally placed. The house has been appropriately furnished and has the look of still being lived in by people of quality.

THE FORD MANSION—c.1774
Morris Street, Morristown, New Jersey

OPEN   Every day except Monday   10 A.M. to 5 P.M.
Open same hours on all holidays except Thanksgiving, Christmas and New Year's Day

ADMISSION   .25 per person.   Children under 12 admitted free if accompanied by an adult
Children under 18 in educational groups free

MAIL ADDRESS   Morristown National Historic Park
P. O. Box 759, Morristown, New Jersey

DIRECTIONS   30 miles from New York. It may be reached via N. J. Route 24 from the North or South, via N. J. Route 32 (U. S. Route 202) also. From the West by N. J. Routes 6, 10, 53 and 32.

HISTORICAL COMMENT

The Mansion was built around 1774 by Col. Jacob Ford, Jr., land-owner, iron manufacturer, and ardent patriot of Morris County. In 1779–80 during the worst winter of the Revolutionary War, General Washington used the Mansion as his headquarters. The building was restored by the National Park Service in 1939, and it now has the same appearance as when first built.

ARCHITECTURAL FEATURES

The house may be termed a "Wooden Palladian Mansion of the Dutch-English transition", with a "Dutch door surviving in a Palladian entrance". In most respects, however, it is of the style developed by Inigo Jones in the seventeenth century in England, a style characterized by a symmetrical facade, a rich cornice, a belt course at the second-floor level, and by a hipped roof. The wide boards on the front elevation, set horizontally with flush joints, simulate a surface of dressed stone.

FURNISHINGS

Among the old Ford Family pieces displayed in the house is the secretary desk used by Washington, three Ford high chests of drawers, and a harpsichord made in 1755 by Jacob Kirckman.

WILLIAM TRENT HOUSE—1719
539 South Warren Street, Trenton, New Jersey

OPEN Monday through Saturday, 10 A.M. to 5 P.M. Sundays, 2 P.M. to 5 P.M. Closed Thanksgiving, Christmas, New Year's Day

ADMISSION Adults .25 Children .10
Servicemen and groups of students—Free

MAIL ADDRESS Trent House Commission
539 South Warren St., Trenton, New Jersey

DIRECTIONS A short taxi ride from the Trenton Station

HISTORICAL COMMENT

William Trent, a native of Inverness, Scotland, emigrated to the Colonies in 1683. A successful merchant in Philadelphia, he purchased in 1714 about 800 acres at "Ye Falls of the Delaware" upon which much of present day Trenton stands. He built this house in 1719 and entered public life in New Jersey, first as Judge of the County, then in 1723 Speaker of the General Assembly, and in 1723 Chief Executive. He died in the house in 1724. Lewis Morris, Colonial Governor of New Jersey, leased the house from 1742 to 1746. Owned by Col. John Cox from 1778–92, it was known as "Bloomsbury Court". The last owner, Mr. Edward A. Stokes, gave the property to the city of Trenton.

ARCHITECTURAL FEATURES

The house was described in the Pennsylvania Journal for March 12, 1767, when it was advertised for sale by its owner, Robert L. Hooper—"it is accommodated with a genteel brick dwelling house 40 x 48 feet, two stories high, four rooms on a floor, with a large handsome staircase and entry, with a cellar under the whole building and a courtyard on each front of the house, one fronting down the River Delaware to the ferry through a large handsome avenue of English cherry trees, the other fronting up the river to Trenton".

FURNISHINGS

The actual inventory taken in 1726, two years after the death of William Trent, is on file in the office of the Superior Court of New Jersey, State House Annex, in a bound volume. It was used as a guide to furnish the house.

SCHUYLER MANSION—1761
Albany, New York

OPEN   Daily 9 A.M. to 5 P.M.
        Sundays 1 P.M. to 5 P.M.

ADMISSION   Free

MAIL ADDRESS   Schuyler Mansion
                Clinton & Catherine Streets
                Albany, New York

DIRECTIONS   Located in downtown Albany at
              Clinton and Catherine Streets

In 1755 Philip Schuyler married Kitty van Rensselaer and in January of 1761, toward the end of the French and Indian War, decided to build the house which was begun in May and completed several years later. In 1755 he was appointed one of four Major-Generals and placed in charge of troops in the North. He was a member of the Continental Congress in 1779–80 and in 1780 helped Washington to reorganize the Army. From 1780 to 1789 he held public office continually. Many visitors were entertained here: Charles Carroll, Washington, Lafayette, Franklin, Talleyrand, Kosciuszko, Aaron Burr, Steuben, Knox, Greene, and many others. In 1911 the mansion was purchased by the State of New York and in 1916 partially restored. Further restoration was carried out and furnishings acquired in 1948.

ARCHITECTURAL FEATURES

Just before the construction of the house, which is a brick building 62 by 48 feet, began, Philip Schuyler went to England to represent Col. John Bradstreet. The house, built in part from lumber from Schuyler's mill and with labor of the Schuyler's slaves, was still unfinished when he returned from England in 1762. Alexander Hamilton, who later married Schuyler's daughter, found "only four rooms finished. . . . no other part of the house was floored except with unplaned boards, so that all the locks, hinges, glass, paper hangings, papier mache, marble chimney pieces, hewn stone steps, and window frames were procured and paid for by Schuyler partly in England and partly after his return."

FURNISHINGS

The walls and woodwork are painted as determined by the exposure of original colors on the paneling. Window and bed hangings are reproductions of eighteenth-century materials woven in silk, wool, cotton and linen. The house contains a wealth of furniture formerly in the possession of the Schuyler family together with books, silver, glass and clothing.

ROCK HALL—1767
Broadway, Lawrence, Long Island

OPEN   Weekdays 10:00 A.M. to 5:00 P.M.   Closed Tuesdays
          Sundays 12:00 Noon to 5:00 P.M.

ADMISSION   Adults .50   Minors accompanied by an adult .25
          Groups from schools, colleges, educational institu-
          tions and from historical and genealogical socie-
          ties free by appointment with custodian.
          Telephone Cedarhurst 9-1157

DIRECTIONS   From New York City go to Lawrence, Long Is-
          land via Queens Blvd., Van Wyck Expressway
          and Rockaway Turnpike. At Lawrence turn
          right on Broadway. About 45 minutes from
          New York City.

HISTORICAL COMMENT

Built in 1767 by Josiah Martin who came to Hempstead from Antigua. He owned many acres of land which extended almost the width of Long Island. After his death in 1778 his heirs lived on in the house until 1824 when it was acquired by the Hewlett family. This was the only other family to occupy the house until 1948 when descendents of the original Hewletts gave it to the town of Hemstead. $130,000 was appropriated by the town for its rehabilitation.

ARCHITECTURAL FEATURES

Rock Hall is painted white with simple vigorous Georgian trim and the typical broad windows. The roof of Rock Hall has a broad and graceful gambrel with a Chinese trellis roof railing. This final blending of the Dutch and English colonial styles produced an architecture of charm and beauty that inherited the best of both traditions. Inside the rooms are beautifully paneled in the style of 1767. As in the case of the Peirce-Nichols House the large drawing room was redecorated for a wedding in the style of 1800.

FURNISHINGS

Among the furnishings are four Chippendale chairs belonging to the original owners of Rock Hall; the traveling tea case of President John Adams; gold candelabra, the property of Joseph Bonaparte; and a bed, press, blanket chest and chairs which were all originally in Rock Hall.

VAN CORTLANDT MANSION—1748

Van Cortlandt Park near 242nd Street, New York, New York

OPEN   Every day

ADMISSION   .25 on Sunday, Monday, Tuesday, and Wednesday. Other days free

MAIL ADDRESS   Department of Parks
New York, New York

DIRECTIONS   Take Broadway Branch of West Side Interborough Subway to 242nd Street. By car, take Yonkers exit of the Henry Hudson Parkway and go south two blocks.

HISTORICAL COMMENT

Frederick van Cortlandt erected this house on the banks of Mosholu Brook in 1748. At that time it was surrounded by a large and very prosperous farm, remaining so until the Revolution. During the entire war, this area was in the midst of all the activity between the British, who occupied New York, and the forces under Washington in Westchester. Sometimes it would be the British who were in the house; at other times, the Americans. Finally, in November 1783, Washington spent the night, and the next day rode to New York to observe the evacuation of the British.

New York City acquired ownership in 1889, and in 1896 it was leased to the Colonial Dames and opened in May 1897.

ARCHITECTURAL FEATURES

The Van Cortlandt Mansion is one of the few examples of Colonial architecture on the grand scale still extant in the New York City area. Built of stone, it has an L plan so that it is one room deep. The carved stone images over the windows of the facade are unique in colonial architecture. The curly maple handrail of the staircase is seldom seen in other houses.

FURNISHINGS

The furnishings contain some excellent examples of furniture of the period of the house as well as some twenty or thirty years earlier and later. It also contains a splendid collection of Dutch Delft and an unusual child's tea set of Wieldon ware.

THE MORRIS-JUMEL MANSION—1765
West 160th Street at Jumel Terrace, New York, New York

OPEN   Every day except Monday 11 A.M. to 5 P.M.

ADMISSION   Free

MAIL ADDRESS   The Morris-Jumel Mansion
West 160th Street at Jumel Terrace, New
York, New York

DIRECTIONS   By car—up St. Nicholas Ave. to 160th Street,
turn right one block
By 5th Avenue Bus—No. 2, No. 3, to 160th Street
By 8th Avenue Subway, AA train to 163rd Street

Roger Morris, after serving as a Captain under General Braddock in the disastrous campaign against the French and Indians, returned to New York. After marrying Mary Philipse in 1758, he served with Wolfe against Quebec. Returning again to New York he built in 1765 the mansion which he called Mount Morris. Col. Morris, a Tory, went to England when the Revolution started and in August of 1776 Mount Morris became General Heath's headquarters. After the Battle of Long Island, General Washington occupied it for a brief period. Later when abandoned to the British, General Sir Henry Clinton occupied it from time to time. After the war it was sold and resold several times. In 1810 Stephen Jumel bought it for $10,000. At his death his widow married Aaron Burr, who lived here. Mme. Jumel entertained Joseph Bonaparte and Louis Napoleon, who became Emperor Napoleon III, during her residence.

ARCHITECTURAL FEATURES

The facade with its four columns, two stories in height, is unusual in a pre-Revolutionary house. One of the post-Colonial features added by the Jumels when they saved the house from ruin in 1810 is the imposing front entrance doorway with flanking side lights and elliptical fanlight. In 1903 after several changes of ownership, the City of New York purchased the property for $235,000 and custodianship was given to the D.A.R. who restored it as a museum.

FURNISHINGS

In furnishing, consideration has been given to the fact that it was occupied by two noted families during widely separated periods; the background of one English, the other French. The styles of the period prior to the Revolution have been combined with American Federal and French Empire.

MORRIS HOUSE—1772

5442 Germantown Ave., Philadelphia, Pennsylvania

OPEN   Daily except Mondays from 2:00 to 5:00 P.M.

ADMISSION   Adults   .25   Children   .10

MAILING ADDRESS   Department of the Interior
National Park Service
5442 Germantown Ave., Philadelphia 44,
Pennsylvania

DIRECTIONS   Nine blocks north of the Wayne Junction station
of the Reading Railroad on Germantown Ave.

HISTORICAL COMMENT

The Morris house was built in 1772 by David Deschler. Several years later, in October 1777, the British Commander, Sir William Howe, set up his headquarters here after the battle of Germantown. Deschler died in his house in 1792 and it was then sold to Col. Isaac Franks. In 1793 yellow fever in Philadelphia forced removal of the officials of the Federal Government to Germantown, and Washington rented this house from Col. Franks for several weeks, during which time many cabinet meetings were held here. Returning on July 30, 1794, the President again occupied the house, remaining until Septembr 20th. Col. Frank's bill, amounting to $201.06, presented on the 20th was paid in full on the 24th. Samuel Morris bought the house in 1834 and it remained in the family until ownership was transferred to the United States Government.

ARCHITECTURAL FEATURES

The Morris House, 45 feet wide and 40 feet deep, is architecturally notable for its 24 paned windows, its massive recessed door and classic doorway, and its beautiful woodwork, both inside and out. The Tidewater paneling of the downstairs hall is unique in houses of its age in this area. The original colors of the woodwork, greys, greens and blues, have been restored to each of the rooms.

FURNISHINGS

The house has been handsomely furnished through private loans as well as the assistance of the Philadelphia Museum of Art.

CEDAR GROVE—1721
Fairmount Park, Philadelphia, Pennsylvania

OPEN Daily including Sundays 10:00 A.M. to 5:00 P.M.
Closed legal holidays

ADMISSION Adults .25   Children .10

MAIL ADDRESS Philadelphia Museum of Art
26th and Parkway, Philadelphia 30, Pa.

DIRECTIONS Located in Fairmount Park just north of Girard
Avenue.

HISTORICAL COMMENT

In 1927 Cedar Grove was taken down stone by stone and removed from its original site at Harrogate near Frankford, where in 1721 after his marriage to Elizabeth Coates, who owned the property, Joseph Paschall built the oldest part. In 1767 the Paschall's son, Isaac, married Patience Mifflin and Cedar Grove was inherited by their daughter Sarah, who married Isaac Wister Morris in 1795. Finally, in 1888, the proximity of factories and railroads obliged the great-great-grandchildren of the Paschalls to vacate Cedar Grove.

ARCHITECTURAL FEATURES

In 1721 Cedar Grove consisted of only three rooms; the parlor (now the dining room), the bedroom above it and the kitchen in the one story extension in the rear. Substantial additions were made in 1752 in the form of a bedroom and attic over the old kitchen. In 1795 the house was doubled in width, providing a parlor, a large kitchen and two more bedrooms and additional attic space.

FURNISHINGS

When Cedar Grove was restored, Miss Lydia Thompson Morris replaced all the furniture that had previously been there. Seldom can one see a house with original pieces exactly as it was when lived in during the eighteenth century.

MOUNT PLEASANT—1762
Fairmount Park, Philadelphia, Pennsylvania

OPEN   Every day including Sunday   10:00 A.M. to 5:00 P.M.
Closed on legal holidays

ADMISSION   Adults .25   Children .10

MAIL ADDRESS   Philadelphia Museum of Art
Philadelphia 30, Pennsylvania

DIRECTIONS   Enter Park from 33rd Street, either at Oxford St.
Columbia Ave., Diamond St. or Dauphin St.

Captain John Macpherson came to Philadelphia from Scotland and in 1757 began privateering. In a few years he had amassed a fortune, using some of it to build Mount Pleasant. His eldest son, John, was aide-de-camp to General Montgomery and fell with his commander-in-chief in the assault on Quebec. In the spring of 1779, General Benedict Arnold bought the house prior to his marriage to Peggy Shippen and after the marriage gave it to her, but neither ever lived there. In 1792 Jonathan Williams, a great-nephew of Benjamin Franklin, bought Mount Pleasant, retaining ownership until 1853. In 1868 it became the property of the city of Philadelphia.

ARCHITECTURAL FEATURES

Mount Pleasant is noteworthy architecturally. It is Philadelphia's finest example of a Colonial gentleman's country seat. Thomas T. Waterman calls it the finest Colonial house north of the Mason and Dixon Line. The plan of the house was probably suggested by a plan by Marot. On the ground floor there is a center hall, with a large drawing room on one side and a smaller dining room and lateral stair hall on the other. Outside, the brick walls have been stuccoed, giving an impression of boldness to the brick quoins at the corner. The Palladian window over the entrance, the pedimented pavilion and the dormers on the roof give the facade great strength of character.

FURNISHINGS

The house is furnished throughout with excellent examples of Philadelphia Chippendale made between 1760 and 1785.

WOODFORD—1756
Fairmount Park, Philadelphia, Pennsylvania

OPEN   Daily except Monday from 1:00 to 5:00 P.M.

ADMISSION   Free

MAIL ADDRESS   Mr. John P. B. Sinkler, Trustee
1500 Walnut Street, Philadelphia, Penn.

DIRECTIONS   Woodford is in the East Park at Dauphin and
33rd Streets.
Telephone: Baldwin 9–6115

HISTORICAL COMMENT

William Coleman, an intimate friend of Benjamin Franklin for over forty years, bought the property in 1756 and completed extensive enlargements to a smaller house of somewhat ealier date. William Coleman was Judge of the Supreme Court from 1759 until his death in 1769. Owned briefly by Alexander Barclay of His Majesty's Customs, Woodford became the home of David Franks, an eminent Jewish merchant, in 1771. Compelled to remove to New York in 1780, his sister Tela married Captain De Lancey and his daughter married Gen. Sir Henry Johnson, who was defeated and captured by Gen. Anthony Wayne at Stony Point. Woodford, in 1780, went to Thomas Paschall and in 1793 to the Wharton family and to the ownership of Fairmount Park in 1868. It was serving as a guard house at the time it was restored, and is furnished with the Naomi Wood collection of antiques.

ARCHITECTURAL FEATURES

Woodford is a "curious and interesting house" which was apparently first a one story house that was raised in 1756 to two stories. Penteaves carry entirely around the house at the second floor level. Its drawing room is one of the finest in Philadelphia.

FURNISHINGS

Woodford is furnished with a collection of very wonderful American furniture which was left by Miss Naomi Wood to be placed in an appropriate house. The extent of the collection is such that it completely furnishes the house and gives a very lived in appearance.

NICHOLS-WANTON-HUNTER HOUSE—1748
54 Washington Street, Newport, Rhode Island

OPEN Every day 10:00 A.M. to 5:00 P.M.
May 15th to October 15th
Open by appointment at other times

ADMISSION Adults 1.00 Children under 16 .25
Servicemen in uniform .50
Students in groups of 5 or more .25

MAIL ADDRESS The Preservation Society of Newport
County
5 Charles Street, Newport, Rhode Island

DIRECTIONS From Washington Square go west on Long Wharf
to Washington Street and turn right two blocks.

In 1748 Deputy Governor Jonathan Nichols, Jr., proprietor of The White Horse Tavern (now in process of restoration), owner of privateers, and prosperous merchant, bought the property and sometime between then and his death in 1754 built the house that now stands, possibly incorporating an earlier structure. The inventory of his personal estate taken in 1756 is in the Newport Historical Society. That same year Col. Joseph Wanton, Jr., Deputy Governor in 1764 and 1767, son of Governor Wanton, bought the house and lived there until 1775, when because of Tory sympathies he went to New York. Following confiscation it was owned by several Providence investors until bought in 1805 by William Hunter, Harvard lawyer, United States Senator and Ambassador to Brazil. Following his death in 1849 it passed through a succession of hands until in 1948 it was purchased by the Preservation Society of Newport County.

ARCHITECTURAL COMMENT

Few if any houses of Colonial America have so much of the early "bolection-moulded" paneling. The two best rooms have pilasters either side of the fireplace and in the four corners of the room, all with magnificently carved Corinthian capitals. The entire interior has been painted as it was originally with three "grained" rooms and one with "marbleized" decoration, offering a rare opportunity to study eighteenth-century painting technique as it existed in the finer houses.

FURNISHINGS

The Preservation Society is gradually furnishing the house with acquisitions of the Newport furniture of the Goddards, Townsends, Holmes Weaver, etc., with the idea of making this a museum devoted entirely to Newport items. In the meantime each summer rare examples of early Newport craftsmanship are exhibited on loan so that the house will present a completely furnished effect.

WANTON-LYMAN-HAZARD HOUSE—c. 1695
Newport, Rhode Island

OPEN   May 15 to October 15
Every day from 10:00 A.M. to 5:00 P.M.

ADMISSION   Adults   .50

MAIL ADDRESS   Preservation Society of Newport County
5 Charles Street, Newport, Rhode Island

DIRECTIONS   On Broadway just north of the Colony House.

HISTORICAL COMMENT

Stephen Mumford probably built this house just prior to 1700. In 1724 he sold it to Richard Ward, who later became Governor of the Colony. In 1765 Martin Howard, Jr., author of the pro-British diatribe "A Letter from a Gentleman at Halifax", was living in the house. In that year when word of the passage of the Stamp Act reached Newport in August, an angry mob attacked Howard's house, where they smashed doors, windows, interiors and furnishings. Howard left town and John Wanton bought the house at auction. Wanton's daughter, Polly, married Daniel Lyman and her father gave them the house. Their daughter, Harriet, married Benjamin Hazard and the house remained in the Hazard family until purchased by the Newport Historical Society in 1927.

ARCHITECTURAL FEATURES

The chimney with its pilastered top is one of very few of this type constructed of brick. The fireplaces, with coves and rounded walls, are typical of early Rhode Island practice. The sharply pitched roof was kicked out across the front to take a huge plaster coved cornice. Inside the framework was originally all exposed and the north chamber has been restored to show the shamfered ceiling beams and the massive gunstock corner posts. The vertical boarding is marbled in a kind of feather treatment in dull red and gray. The front door, the sash windows and the fireplace paneling are all eighteenth century additions.

FURNISHINGS

There are many fine pieces of the Townsend-Goddard era together with some that date earlier.

CARRINGTON HOUSE—1812
66 William Street, Providence, Rhode Island

OPEN Every day Tuesday through Sunday 1 P.M. to 5 P.M.
Closed Christmas and the 4th of July

ADMISSION Free

MAIL ADDRESS Museum of Art, Rhode Island School of Design
Providence 3, Rhode Island

DIRECTIONS A short taxi ride from Union Station
By Car—City Hall Park via Waterman Street to
Benefit Street, turn right—go to Williams
Street, turn left and go one block

HISTORICAL CONNECTION

Built by John Corlis in 1812, the house was bought within a year by Edward Carrington, a prominent shipping merchant, and it remained in the family until 1936 when it was given to the Rhode Island School of Design.

Edward Carrington had just returned from China, where he served as American Consul and while he never returned to China, he maintained an active interest in the China trade and lived surrounded by many objects of Oriental origin, most of which remain in the house today.

ARCHITECTURAL FEATURES

While it is a mansion of the so-called Federal or Republican design, both inside and out it retains features reminiscent of the style of fifty or more years earlier. The southeast parlor retains some of the serene charm of the Colonial period. Upstairs the northeast bedroom with adjoining dressing rooms offered the spacious luxury which had by 1812 become a part of the finer residences.

FURNITURE

The Chinese wallpaper made in China to Carrington's specification and the paper made by the Dufours Company in France during the first quarter of the nineteenth century are notable; the former for its birds and flowers, the latter for its portrayal of the exotic land of India. Furniture is both American and Chinese, blending together in a manner reminiscent of the life of its original owner.

JOHN BROWN HOUSE—1786
52 Power Street, Providence, Rhode Island

OPEN   Monday through Friday, 9 A.M. to 5 P.M.
Sunday 3 to 5 P.M.
Closed holidays and holiday week-ends, and on Sundays during June, July and August

ADMISSION   Free

MAIL ADDRESS   John Brown House, 52 Power Street
Providence, Rhode Island

DIRECTIONS   From Memorial Square go up to Waterman Street to Benefit Street, turn right and go on Benefit to Power Street, then turn left

HISTORICAL COMMENT

John Brown House was built in 1786 by John Brown, third of the famous four Brown brothers (Nicholas, Joseph, John, and Moses), merchants of Providence. John was the organizer of the plan to burn the British ship *Gaspee* when it ran aground in Narragansett Bay, while enforcing the revenue acts. A leader in the shipping trade to the southern colonies and the Indies, he was active in many other commercial ventures. His Hope Furnace provided the iron for the fence that still stands at the Battery in New York. His home was visited by Mrs. John Adams in 1789 and by George Washington in 1790. He and his brothers were instrumental in establishing Rhode Island College (now Brown University) in Providence.

ARCHITECTURAL FEATURES

Joseph Brown, Professor of Natural Philosophy, designed the house in the Georgian style, but died before the work began in 1786. The original house is 54 x 50 feet. (The ell was added at a later date.) Three stories high with an attic, it is one of the most highly developed examples of its style in America.

The lavish detail of the interior woodwork, the extensive use of mahogany for the doors and trim and the staircases of the central halls, set it apart as one of the most beautiful houses along the Atlantic seaboard.

FURNISHINGS

Serving as the home of The Rhode Island Historical Society, it has both a museum and a library with the principal rooms furnished with fine examples of American furniture (many of the Newport school) and paintings of the eighteenth century. The nine shell desk and bookcase by John Goddard and a self portrait of Robert Feke and his wife are features.

GOV. STEPHEN HOPKINS HOUSE—1707–42

Corner of Hopkins & Benefit Streets, Providence, Rhode Island

OPEN   Wednesdays and Saturdays 1 to 4 P.M.
        Also open by appointment for special groups

ADMISSION   Free

MAIL ADDRESS   Stephen Hopkins House
                Hopkins & Benefit Sts., Providence, Rhode
                Island

DIRECTIONS   From Memorial Square go up Waterman Street
              to Benefit Street, turn right and proceed south
              on Benefit Street two blocks to Hopkins Street

HISTORICAL COMMENT

Stephen Hopkins was born March 7, 1707, in Cranston, R. I. He married a Quaker, Sarah Scott, when he was 19 and they had 7 children. A self-educated man, he helped found the Public Library. He was Chief Justice of the Superior Court, first Chancellor of Brown University, ten times Governor of Rhode Island, a member of the First Continental Congress, and a Signer of the Declaration of Independence. Sixty-nine at the time and afflicted with palsy, he said as he signed the document "my hand trembles but my heart does not". He was host to Washington in Providence the same year. At his death in 1785 he freed all his slaves.

ARCHITECTURAL FEATURES

The house now known as the Stephen Hopkins house was built in 1707, consisting of 2 rooms and an unfinished attic. Hopkins bought the house in 1742, adding the other rooms in 1743. In 1804 it was moved half way up the hill from a location now the corner of Hopkins and South Main Streets. In 1927 it was moved to its present location, where it was restored under the direction of Norman Isham; the fireplaces and chimneys are original, as are the floors except the keeping room and first floor bedroom. The shell cupboard over the fireplace in the parlor is distinctive of Rhode Island and is a superlative accomplishment in interior design.

FURNISHINGS

The furnishings include a silver porringer marked SSH for Stephen and Sarah Hopkins together with appropriate furniture of the period, for the most part gifts of the Colonial Dames of Rhode Island.

SHIRLEY—1723–1740
Route 2, Charles City, Virginia

OPEN Daily (including holidays) 9 A.M. to 5 P.M.

ADMISSION Adults 1.00   Children .50
Student Groups   .40 per person

MAIL ADDRESS Route 2, Charles City, Virginia

DIRECTIONS Located on Route 5 between Williamsburg and
Richmond

HISTORICAL COMMENT

Edward Hill the third, builder of the present house, 1723–1740, was a member of the House of Burgesses and Collector of the Revenue. He married Elizabeth Williams, daughter of Sir Edward Williams of Wales and the owner of North Wales. Edward Hill's daughter inherited Shirley and married John Carter, son of Robert "King" Carter. Ann Hill Carter was married to "Light Horse" Harry Lee at Shirley. Among their children was Robert E. Lee who frequently visited the home of his mother. Shirley is one of the very few Colonial homes that still remain in the original family.

ARCHITECTURAL FEATURES

While tradition places the date of Shirley as between 1723–1740, Thomas T. Waterman in *Mansions of Virginia* expresses the opinion that the mansard roof and porticos were not additions of about 1830 but that it was built as a whole around 1765. Regardless of which date is right, its exterior is monumental and is strongly Palladian in appearance. The interior is notable for many reasons; the great expanse of paneling, the magnificent staircase, the drawing room chimney piece, and the trim of the windows are among the most important.

FURNISHINGS

The furnishings are the accumulation of many generations and present an almost unique opportunity to observe the history of its occupants over many, many years. A rare opportunity which should not be missed.

MONTICELLO — 1769–1809
Charlottesville, Virginia

OPEN 8 A.M. to 5 P.M. Daily every day in the year

ADMISSION Single admission .90   Servicemen in uniform .30
Adults in groups (15 or more) .30   University of
Virginia students with identification .30   Elemen-
tary and high school students in groups of 15 or
more .30   Children under 12 with parents free

MAIL ADDRESS Thomas Jefferson Memorial Foundation, Inc.
Box 316, Charlottesville, Virginia

DIRECTIONS There are numerous road signs throughout Virginia that mark the route well. It is 3 miles south
of Charlottesville on Route 20, then Route 53.

HISTORICAL COMMENT

Designed and built under the personal supervision of Thomas Jefferson (1743–1826), a graduate of William and Mary College in 1762. At the age of 33 he was author of the Declaration of Independence and later President of the United States, 1801–1809. He had been Secretary of State from 1790 to 1793. After his second term as President, he retired to Monticello and spent the last 16 years of his life there. People from all over the world came to see him. A man of great versatility, he was in addition to statesman and diplomat, administrator, planter, architect, lawyer, author and philosopher. His inventive nature resulted in many unique features in his home. He and John Adams both died July 4, 1826, the 50th anniversary of the Declaration of Independence.

ARCHITECTURAL FEATURES

Begun in 1769, Monticello was not completed until 1809, due to enlargements and remodeling. Many of the bricks, nails, and much hardware were made on the property and the timbers hewn there. Unique features include the seven-day clock in the entrance hall, a dumb-waiter concealed in the dining room mantel and specially built beds. He was a life-long admirer of Andrea Palladio, whose Roman country house style was the basis for his own style, which when executed in the brick and white wood trim, had a distinctly Virginia flavor.

FURNISHINGS

Monticello has been fortunate in recovering many of the original furnishings including some of Jefferson's own design, such as his work table and filing table. The revolving chair was ordered from abroad and was the first of its kind in America. The table in front of the chair was designed by him. Some of the furnishings are French as they were in his day. The curtains are made from original sketches executed by Jefferson.

KENMORE—1752

1201 Washington Ave., Fredericksburg, Virginia

OPEN Every day in the year except Christmas, Thanksgiving and New Year's Day   Nov. 15 to Feb. 28—9 A.M. to 4:30 P.M.
Mar. 1 to Nov. 14—8:30 A.M. to 5 P.M.

ADMISSION   Adults .60   Children 10 to 16 .45   Members of the Armed Forces free (in uniform)   Special rates for special groups   Admission includes tea and gingerbread in Kenmore kitchen

MAIL ADDRESS   "Kenmore", Washington Avenue
Fredericksburg, Virginia

DIRECTIONS   Fredericksburg is 52 miles from Washington D.C. and 56 miles from Richmond. Routes U.S. 1 and 17 follow Princess Ann Street through Fredericksburg —turn west on William Street—5 blocks to Washington Street, then two and a half blocks north

The mansion on the Kenmore estate was built in 1752 by Fielding Lewis for his bride, Betty Washington, the sister of General Washington. Colonel Lewis was prominent in the Revolution and at his own expense manufactured, in large quantities, arms and ammunition. The large sums he advanced so impoverished his estate that "Kenmore" was lost to the Lewis family through their own patriotism. The roster of guests at Kenmore is imposing: Washington, Rochambeau, Mercer, John Paul Jones, Patrick Henry, Thomas Jefferson, and George Mason, to mention only a few. The Kenmore Association formed in 1922 saved the historic house and is responsible for its restoration.

ARCHITECTURAL FEATURES

Thomas T. Waterman, writing in *The Mansions of Virginia*, says of "Kenmore"—"the simplicity of the exterior is in contrast to the elaborate decoration of the interior. The impression of richness of the interior is largely due to the superb plaster relief ceilings and over mantels that probably date from shortly after 1770. . . . The earlier trim may comprise all the present woodwork except perhaps the fine carved mantels. . . . Its interiors are superb examples of Virginia Georgian at its best."

FURNISHINGS

Its furnishings, meticulously authentic and luxurious in scope, include some that originally belonged in the Lewis family. The combination of the high quality of the house itself and the furnishings make this one of the best of the best.

GUNSTON HALL—1755
Lorton, Virginia

OPEN   Every day of the year except Christmas
The hours are 9:30 A.M. to 5:00 P.M. Washington D. C.
Time   Annual Memorial Celebration—June 12th

ADMISSION Adults .50   High School Children .25
Younger children, free   Servicemen in uniform, free
Groups of 20 or more, half price

MAIL ADDRESS Director, Gunston Hall, Lorton, Virginia

DIRECTIONS Entrance on Route 1, junction with Route 242,
25 miles south of Washington; or at Lorton on
Shirley Highway

HISTORICAL COMMENT

Gunston Hall was the home of George Mason (1725–92), the fourth generation in Virginia to bear that name; the author in 1774 of the "Fairfax Resolves", the first statement of the rights of the Colonies; friend, advisor and neighbor of Washington. He wrote the Virginia Declaration of Rights adopted in Williamsburg June 12, 1776. In the preamble appears for the fiirst time the phrase "Life, Liberty, and the pursuit of Happiness". The body is the basis for the Bill of Rights—the first ten amendments to our Constitution. He was author of the Virginia Constitution, the first drawn up in the Colonies. He is buried beside his wife within the shadows of the house he built.

ARCHITECTURAL FEATURES

The architect, William Buckland, who afterward designed the Hammond-Harwood House at Annapolis, came to America from London specifically to build this house. From the outside the house is graceful but neither large nor imposing. The interior however is one of the most impressive to be found in any house of our Colonial era. Observe two rooms in particular, the one executed using a Chinese Chippendale design and, the other, the Palladian drawing room. These are masterpieces of design and craftmanship.

FURNISHINGS

Each year the amount and quality of the furnishings have improved, approaching the perfection which the custodians have in mind. The dining table, an unusually large oval one, with six legs with claw-and-ball feet, is one of the very finest known.

MOUNT VERNON—1743—1759—1773
Mount Vernon, Virginia

OPEN   Open every day in the year
March 1 to October 1   9 A.M. to 5 P.M.
October 1 to March 1   9 A.M. to 4 P.M.

ADMISSION   Adults .50   Children under 12 free
Servicemen in uniform free
School children when chaperoned free

MAIL ADDRESS   Mount Vernon Ladies Association of the Union
Mount Vernon, Virginia

DIRECTIONS   Reached from Washington via Alexandria and
the Mount Vernon Memorial Highway, a distance of 12 miles. Coming from the south on
Route U.S. 1, take State Highway 235.

It is not known whether the present Mansion was begun by George Washington's father, Augustine, or his elder half-brother, Lawrence, who occupied it in 1743. At Lawrence's death in 1752, title passed to George. After 5 years spent in active military service against the French and Indians, he returned and married in 1759, Martha Custis, widow of Daniel P. Custis, taking up their residence at Mount Vernon that Spring. During the eight years, 1775 to 1783, while serving as Commander-in-Chief of the American forces he visited Mount Vernon only twice. On his return he completed the enlargement, which had been supervised in his absence by Lund Washington. Six years later he became President of the United States and was absent eight more years, 1789–1797. He died here on December 14, 1799. In 1853 this historic shrine was saved from destruction by the Mount Vernon Ladies Association of the Union. For over one hundred years this organization has devoted its efforts to the preservation and proper furnishing of this most historic house.

ARCHITECTURAL FEATURES

Prior to his marriage in 1759, Washington planned the modifications that were to make an important mansion out of a modest dwelling. The house was raised from one and one-half stories to two and one-half stories and extensively redecorated. In 1773, Washington made plans for additions to each end of the "Great House". These additions, the end buildings and connecting colonnades, were completed during his absence with the Continental Army. On his return, much remained to be done to bring it to the state in which the visitor now sees it. Not until 1787 was the final embellishment, the weather vane, set in place.

FURNISHINGS

Year after year by purchase, donation, and bequest, the original furnishings are being acquired. At the present time most of the pieces on the first floor and all of those in Washington's bedroom are original.

WOODLAWN PLANTATION—1805
Mount Vernon, Virginia

OPEN   Every day except Christmas and New Year's Day
Closed Monday November through February
March through October   10:00 A.M. to 5:00 P.M.
November through February   10:00 A.M. to 4:30 P.M.

ADMISSION   Adults   .50
Free to children under 14 and service personnel in uniform.
Group rates available.

MAIL ADDRESS   Woodlawn Plantation
Mount Vernon, Virginia

DIRECTIONS   13 miles south of Washington on U. S. Route 1.

HISTORICAL COMMENT

Woodlawn Plantation was built by Lawrence Lewis, the son of Fielding and Betty Washington Lewis of Kenmore, on a 2,000 acre tract which was part of the original Mount Vernon estate. The land was given him and his wife, Nelly Custis, a granddaughter of Martha Washington, as a wedding present when they were married on Washington's last birthday in 1799. The young couple had met at Mount Vernon, following the General's retirement, when Major Lewis came to act as secretary to his uncle. Mrs. Lewis had grown up there and had been adopted by Washington. William Thornton was the architect of Woodlawn, and probably drew upon suggestions of his friend Washington, who had chosen the site. The Lewises moved from Mount Vernon in 1802 after Mrs. Washington's death. At that time only the two wings were completed. The Lewises sold the property in 1846. By 1900 the property was falling into ruin, but a succession of owners restored the mansion. Senator Oscar W. Underwood of Alabama, and Mrs. Underwood, were the last private owners. In 1951 the property was turned over to the National Trust for Historic Preservation for administration, by the Woodlawn Public Foundation, Inc., which had saved the property as an historic site.

ARCHITECTURAL FEATURES

Dr. William Thornton, the first architect of the United States Capitol, of the Octagon House, and of Tudor Place, the residence of Mrs. Lewis' sister Mrs. Peter, designed a late Georgian residence which is notable for its river portico, the Aquia stone trim, and the fact that, unlike most great plantation houses, it housed under one roof all functions of living. The large, airy rooms and big windows are of Thornton's finest design. The staircase and grained-painted woodwork are most interesting and beautiful.

FURNISHINGS

Woodlawn Mansion is furnished with many possessions of the Lewises, and furniture of the Hepplewhite, Sheraton and early Empire style.

WILTON—1753
South Wilton Road, Richmond Virginia

OPEN   Weekdays   9:00 A.M. to 5:00 P.M.

Sundays   3:00 P.M. to 5:00 P.M.

Closed Sundays from July 1st until after Labor Day

Closed National Holidays

ADMISSION   Free, except during Garden Week when the Garden Club of Virginia gets $1.00 per visitor (tax incl.)

MAIL ADDRESS   "Wilton", South Wilton Road, Richmond 26, Virginia

DIRECTIONS   To reach "Wilton" from any Richmond Hotel, drive West on Main Street which becomes Elwood Avenue to end of street, turn left one block to Cary Street Road, turn right on Cary Street Road and continue to end of 5300 block, turn left on South Wilton Road and go to end.

HISTORICAL COMMENT

Verification of the construction date is written behind the cornice in the southwest bedroom—"Sampson Darrell put up this Cornish in the year of our Lord 1753". William Randolph III was the original owner. He had married in 1735 Anne Carter Harrison, daughter of Benjamin Harrison of Berkeley. Washington stopped here while attending the Second Virginia Convention in Richmond in 1775. Thomas Jefferson, whose mother was a Randolph, often visited his Wilton cousins. In 1932, surrounded by factories, it was saved by the Virginia Society of Colonial Dames and moved to its present site.

ARCHITECTURAL FEATURES

Wilton is unique among existing early Virginia houses in that it is panelled throughout and is praised by T. T. Waterman as a "rich study in the final phases of that great period of English woodwork that Wren inaugurated nearly 100 years before".

FURNISHINGS

An early Randolph inventory has been of assistance in selecting the furnishings, all of the eighteenth century, which are constantly being augmented to present a more complete picture of its original appearance.

STRATFORD HALL—1725–1730
Westmoreland County, Virginia

OPEN   Every day 9:00 A.M. to 5:00 P.M., except Christmas

ADMISSION Adults .50   Children .25
Reduced rates for groups of 25 or more
Lunch is on sale from April 15 to October 15

MAIL ADDRESS Stratford Hall
Westmoreland County, Virginia

DIRECTIONS It is 42 miles east of Fredericksburg. Take State Route 3, and turn off at sign pointing to Stratford.
It is 82 miles from Washington via Potomac River Bridge.

Stratford was built by Thomas Lee during the five year period 1725–1730. He received a bounty of three hundred pounds from Her Majesty, Queen Caroline, who was acting as regent in 1729, and applied these funds to the cost of Stratford. In 1732 the third son of Thomas and Hannah (Ludwell) Lee, Richard Henry Lee, was born here. A signer of the Declaration of Independence, ardent patriot, President of the First Continental Congress, he signed the Treaty of Alliance with France, and remained active in public life until his death in 1794. In 1734 Francis Lightfoot Lee was born at Stratford. He also signed the Declaration of Independence and was a member of the Continental Congress, serving his country in many diverse capacities prior to his death in 1797.

In 1750, when Thomas Lee died, Stratford descended to Philip Ludwell Lee, the eldest son. Philip married Elizabeth Steptoe and Stratford descended to their daughter Matilda in 1775, who married her cousin Henry Lee, known as "Light Horse Harry" Lee. He eulogized Washington with the famous words, "First in War, First in Peace and First in the Hearts of his Countrymen". Stratford descended to him at his wife's death in 1790, then to his son in 1808, and was owned by several others prior to its acquisition in 1929 by the Robert E. Lee Memorial Foundation, Inc.

ARCHITECTURAL FEATURES

No structural changes had ever been made in the buildings. Slight additions have been removed and Stratford is today essentially the same as when built by Thomas Lee.

FURNISHINGS

Stratford has been furnished in accordance with inventories at the Courthouse at Montiose. Furniture that originally belonged to the Lee's is gradually being acquired.

BRUSH-EVERARD HOUSE—1717
Williamsburg, Virginia

OPEN   Daily from 10 A.M. to 5 P.M.
       April 1st to October 1st, open at 9 A.M.

		Adults	Students	Military
ADMISSION	8 buildings	3.00	1.50	1.50
	5 buildings	2.50	1.00	1.00
	Brush Everard (only) .75			

MAIL ADDRESS   Colonial Williamsburg
               Williamsburg, Virginia

DIRECTIONS   Williamsburg is 50 miles from Richmond by car
             via Route 60. For more information see Wythe
             House.

HISTORICAL COMMENT

The house was built in 1717 by John Brush, gunsmith, armorer, and first keeper of the Colony's ammunition magazine on Market Square. It was purchased in 1742 by William Dering, dancing teacher at the College of William and Mary, who "conducted the balls and assemblies at the Capitol". The next owner was Thomas Everard, Clerk of York County, 1745–1784, and in 1766 Mayor of Williamsburg. Everard was a gentleman of standing in the community, though less celebrated than George Wythe and others of his friends.

ARCHITECTURAL FEATURES

The two wings which were added in the rear give an unusual U-shaped plan. There is only one other example in Williamsburg. The staircase, with turned balusters and carved step brackets, is remarkable in a house of this size. Fragments of wall papers found in the house have been reproduced and used in several rooms.

FURNISHINGS

The great care and good taste and judgment used in the furnishing have produced a very strong flavor of the eighteenth century. Note particularly the rugs, the antique fabrics and the fine window hangings. The collection of china and pottery in the dining room is superb. There is much furniture of southern origin.

WYTHE HOUSE—1755
Williamsburg, Virginia

		Adults	Students	Military
OPEN	Daily from 10 A.M. to 5 P.M. April 1st to October 1st open at 9 A.M.			
ADMISSION	8 buildings	3.00	1.50	1.50
	5 buildings	2.50	1.00	1.00
	Wythe House	.75		

OPEN Daily from 10 A.M. to 5 P.M.
   April 1st to October 1st open at 9 A.M.

ADMISSION

MAIL ADDRESS Colonial Williamsburg
     Williamsburg, Virginia

DIRECTIONS Williamsburg is 55 miles from Richmond by car
     via Route 60. Three trains each way per day:
     Leave Richmond 8:30 A.M.–2:35 P.M.–6:50 P.M.
     Leave Williamsburg 10:00 A.M.–3:55 P.M.–8:40 P.M.

George Wythe attended William and Mary College and was one of the foremost classical scholars in Virginia. Admitted to the bar at 20, he married the next year Ann Lewis, who died one year later. In 1754, he moved to Williamsburg and married Elizabeth Taliaferro (pronounced Tolliver). He was an intimate friend of Governors Fauquier and Botetourt, supported Richard Henry Lee's resolution for independence and signed the Declaration of Independence. A friend and teacher of Jefferson, who visited him at his house, he was the first professor of law in America. Poisoned by his nephew, he died in 1806. His house served as Washington's Headquarters prior to the siege of Yorktown and Rochambeau stayed there afterward.

ARCHITECTURAL FEATURES

It is interesting to note the pleasing effect produced by the windows on the second floor, smaller than those on the first, but with an equal number of panes of glass. The severity of the exterior lines is relieved by the horizontal brick lines at the first and the second floor levels. Note also the size and location of the chimneys, providing for eight fireplaces. The stepped brick work at the top (corbeling) is an important feature and contributes much to the exterior design.

FURNISHINGS

The house has been furnished by using inventories of similar houses as a guide. The rare set of flower prints on the stair wall is typical of the eighteenth century. Note the floor covering in the bedrooms and the great variety of eighteenth-century accessories.

DUTTON HOUSE—1782
Shelburne Museum, Inc., Shelburne, Vermont

OPEN   Daily from 9:00 A.M. to 5:00 P.M.

ADMISSION   Adults $1.75   Children   .50 (Complete Tour)
Also group rates

MAIL ADDRESS   Shelburne Museum, Inc.
Shelburne, Vermont

DIRECTIONS   Shelburne is 7 miles south of Burlington on Route
7.

HISTORICAL COMMENT

This Vermont version of the earlier New England Saltbox type was built in 1782 by Salmon Dutton who came from Massachusetts and settled in Cavendish, Vermont. Several years ago it was dismantled and re-erected at its present site.

ARCHITECTURAL FEATURES

As in the earlier houses, the entrance hall is small and in it the stairs rise steeply beside the large central chimney. In several of the rooms stenciling was discovered under layers of wallpaper and it was reproduced when the original could not be saved when it was moved. The kitchen is large and was designed to accommodate the many tasks that were performed therein.

FURNISHINGS

In the furnishing of the house it has been assumed that successive generations would each be responsible for items of their day, taking their places in the house and remaining there together with the earlier pieces. As a result, a superb early ball-foot desk is placed in the same room with early nineteenth-century primitive paintings. In the house are to be found some of the best seventeenth-century New England pieces known.

AMERICANA IN INSTITUTIONS

Over a very long period of time, museums, historical societies, and other similar institutions have been acquiring Americana. Probably upwards of ninety per cent of these collections are now housed in the Fifty Institutions listed. Some of the collections are rich in paintings; others in furniture, silver, furnished period rooms; or in groups of buildings. In recent years, institutions, different from the historical societies and museums, have been established and are now open to the public. The hundreds of thousands of visitors each year is evidence of the public interest. The very brief description that follows will serve to give you basic information about these institutions.

WINTERTHUR

If you have never seen the Henry Francis du Pont Winterthur Museum, you have missed the most thrilling and satisfying experience in the field of Americana. Ever since its opening in November of 1951, sixty people a day have been privileged to see this greatest of all collections of American furniture and furnishings arranged in a hundred period rooms covering the period from 1640 to 1840. The meticulous care and infinite pains taken during its formative period has continued during its administration as a public museum. Highly trained guides are assigned to visitors; one guide to every four visitors. It is therefore necessary to write in advance and receive a ticket "reserved" for a specific hour on a specific day. The admission charge of $1.25 per half day includes guide service.

There are two methods of seeing the hundred rooms Winterthur offers: if you can spend the night in Wilmington, see half one day and half the next; otherwise, see it all in one day. In the spring, usually for six weeks in April and May, the Museum is open without reservation. At that time you see twenty of the most important rooms, as well as special exhibits and the azalea gardens. This would be a good way to make your first visit, but you will be sure to want to return for the full tour on a reserved ticket.

Because of unforeseen circumstances, some of those who have reserved tickets are sometimes forced to change the date, which the Museum will do. The time released then becomes available to those who want to go on short notice. If you cannot plan far ahead, call or write the Museum regarding the availability of getting in on a cancellation.

WILLIAMSBURG

Williamsburg is so well known that little can be told to anyone who has not been there, that he has not already heard from friends or relatives. On the average, about one thousand per day go through the buildings of this restored eighteenth-century Virginia town. Some of the buildings are old, some have been reproduced. Here one finds the variety that goes with any complete settlement: government buildings, shops, homes, and taverns. Each is superbly furnished with antique furniture of both American and English origin. So many facets of early life in America are represented that families find things of interest to all age groups. The atmosphere of peaceful, quiet living is welcomed by visitors who have just left the tensions of the twentieth century.

OLD DEERFIELD VILLAGE

Old Deerfield Village is all on one street, a mile long, with giant elms extending the entire length. The street, the trees, the houses, and the surrounding country are all completely unspoiled. Of all the 500 towns and villages of Colonial New England, Deerfield has changed the least. To walk that mile and go inside the houses is to immerse one's self in the past and feel in every sense the rural New England of two hundred years ago.

OLD MYSTIC SEAPORT

Shipping played a dominant part in the early development of America. Old Mystic Seaport preserves in Connecticut a small segment of one of the many seaports that lined the Atlantic Coast from Maine to Florida. Today the visitor walks down an old street to the wharf and boards the vessels that sailed long before the days of coal, oil, or atomic energy.

SHELBURNE MUSEUM, INC.

Vermont has been justly famous for many years as an ideal place for summer vacations and more recently for winter skiing. Nostalgia comes easily to one who has enjoyed this state, its covered bridges, white church spires, its country stores. Shelburne Museum is preserving examples of each of these, together with a lighthouse, a sidewheel steamer, a collection of carriages, and many other components of the Vermont scene that either have disappeared or may disappear.

THE HENRY FORD MUSEUM & GREENFIELD VILLAGE

In Dearborn, Michigan, a museum and an assembled village function side by side. The museum not only has American furniture, silver, and glass, but also a vast collection of nineteenth-century machines and scientific apparatus. The buildings of the village are placed around a typical New England green; many have associations with nineteenth-century personalities, such as Luther Burbank and H. J. Heinz, while others go back to the eighteenth century.

THE FARMERS MUSEUM

In Cooperstown, New York, the Farmers Museum has assembled farm and handicraft tools, as well as buildings housing a print shop, doctor's office, pharmacy, and lawyer's office. Here one can see how those who lived close to the soil spent their days.

STURBRIDGE VILLAGE

Just over the Connecticut line in central Massachusetts has been assembled a group of houses, shops, and other buildings of the period just after 1810. Occupying a site of superb beauty, these buildings recreate a village of that time. Inside some of the buildings are to be found large collections of hardware, tools, and other items.

CORNING GLASS MUSEUM

The Corning Museum each year intrigues thousands of visitors with displays and demonstrations of the art of glass-making. The story told here is not confined alone to America's efforts in this field of manufacture but includes as well hundreds of years prior to our first glass establishment.

NEW-YORK HISTORICAL SOCIETY *Prentis Collection*

THE FIFTY INSTITUTIONS

CALIFORNIA
☐ *Los Angeles* Los Angeles County Museum
CONNECTICUT
☐ *Hartford* Wadsworth Atheneum
☐ *Hartford* Connecticut Historical Society
☐ *Mystic* Old Mystic Seaport
☐ *New Haven* Yale University Art Gallery
☐ *New Haven* New Haven Historical Society
DELAWARE
☐ *Wilmington* The Henry Francis du Pont Winterthur Museum
DISTRICT OF COLUMBIA
☐ *Washington* National Gallery of Art
☐ *Washington* The Smithsonian Institution
ILLINOIS
☐ *Chicago* Art Institute of Chicago
MARYLAND
☐ *Baltimore* Maryland Historical Society
☐ *Baltimore* Baltimore Museum of Art
MASSACHUSETTS
☐ *Andover* Andover Gallery of Art
☐ *Boston* Museum of Fine Arts
☐ *Boston* Massachusetts Historical Society
☐ *Boston* Boston Athenaeum
☐ *Cambridge* Fogg Museum of Art
☐ *Concord* Concord Antiquarian Society
☐ *Deerfield* Old Deerfield Village
☐ *Salem* Essex Institute
☐ *Salem* Peabody Museum
☐ *Springfield* Springfield Museum of Art
☐ *Sturbridge* Sturbridge Village
☐ *Worcester* American Antiquarian Society
☐ *Worcester* Worcester Art Museum
MICHIGAN
☐ *Dearborn* Henry Ford Museum and Greenfield Village
☐ *Detroit* The Detroit Institute of Arts
MINNESOTA
☐ *Minneapolis* The Minneapolis Institute of Art

MISSOURI
☐ *Kansas City* The William Rockhill Nelson Gallery of Art
☐ *St. Louis* City Art Museum of St. Louis
NEW JERSEY
☐ *Newark* Newark Museum
NEW YORK
☐ *Albany* Albany Museum
☐ *Brooklyn* The Brooklyn Museum of Art
☐ *Cooperstown* The Farmers' Museum
☐ *Corning* The Corning Glass Museum
☐ *New York* New York Historical Society
☐ *New York* Museum of the City of New York
☐ *New York* The Metropolitan Museum of Art
☐ *New York* Cooper Union for the Advancement of Science & Art
OHIO
☐ *Cleveland* Cleveland Museum of Art
☐ *Toledo* Toledo Art Museum
PENNSYLVANIA
☐ *Philadelphia* Philadelphia Museum of Art
☐ *Philadelphia* Historical Society of Pennsylvania
☐ *Philadelphia* The Pennsylvania Academy of the Fine Arts
RHODE ISLAND
☐ *Newport* Newport Historical Society
☐ *Providence* Rhode Island Historical Society
☐ *Providence* Rhode Island School of Design Museum
SOUTH CAROLINA
☐ *Charleston* The Charleston Museum
VIRGINIA
☐ *Richmond* Virginia Museum of Fine Arts
☐ *Williamsburg* Colonial Williamsburg

PHOTOGRAPH CREDITS

Cover, L. E. Tilley, Gilbert Ask, Mount Vernon Ladies Association.
Library of Congress, 12, 20, 24, 28, 30, 42, 48, 58, 66, 74, 80, 98.
Metropolitan Museum, 16, 50, 52, 54.
J. H. Schaefer & Son, 18.
Marblehead Historical Society, 26.
National Park Service, 36, 42, 56, 68.
Haskell, 38.
Antiques Magazine, 62, 64.
Gottscho-Schleiser, 64.
John Hopf, 76, 78.
Thomas F. Scott, 100.
Virginia Chamber of Commerce, 90.

Date Due

		PRINTED	IN U. S. A.